Is There Anything Left for the Rest of Us?

Oliver Baxxter

FIRST EDITION
ISBN: 9798732680294

@oliverbaxxter
www.oliverbaxxter.com

for Jimmy,
wakatepe

subject warning: sex-death-depression-suicide

youth

To Watch a Flower Bloom

it was "quit crying like a little bitch," or no,
maybe it was "quit bitching like a little girl"
and a pat on the shoulder
from a heavy, calloused hand
advice he'd gifted me
once on my 9th birthday
and a few other less celebrated,
less effective times

I wanted to be a strong man
like Hulk Hogan, like James Bond,
like my father
but those men didn't cry when their pet
rabbit died
or forget to bring sunscreen to the pool
spending the next day
hissing at anyone that came near
so I learned to swallow the words
as they swirled behind my teeth
and broke all of my own bones
before anyone else had the chance

I wasn't a strong man
it tore me apart
and before I could change,
he passed away

a small funeral
but they kept the casket open
when I placed my hand on his face
it was stern and cold,
yet unfamiliar
with no one there
reminding me to dry my eyes
before my mom saw,
I cried

I cried until my face turned blue
ashamed, as the tears
sank deep into my fathers' suit

Loyalty Only Lies in Food

in the trailer park that raised me,
there was an old man
that slept in the laundry room
and fed the cats scraps
collected from trash cans
on the Vegas strip

in turn, they kept his body warm
on cold desert nights

unwanted, disregarded
yet loved, regardless

he left each day
before the sun could warm the pavement
and the cats left with him
the oven in the sky would ding,
porch lights on
he'd return
unroll his sleeping bag on the floor
and proceed to feed his mangy,
semi-hairless feline friends

I watched him
through the crack in our
tiny kitchen window
every night, until we moved

I never knew his name
but saw his face whenever
I'd scrape my food into the trash
 and on some nights,
I felt his belly rumble
deep within my own
so I'd shovel the rest of it down

and every time I see a cat,
I can't help but wonder if
they know I know their secret

1. on the first of the month
my mom would wake me up
before the sun
could heat the cracked sidewalks
to catch a bus
downtown

I loved people watching
on public transportation
everyone looked lost
but eventually got off
somewhere
my father once told me,
that the only people who race the sun
were trying to outrun themselves
and I guess that's why everyone
always looked so tired

mom and I would split a pack of Pop-Tarts
that'd I'd chew with the sides of my mouth
on account of my two front teeth
still figuring it out

I liked to save the wrappers
one, because name brands were important to
me and *two*, because the plastic
was shiny

30 minutes later we'd get off
and get in line
behind the others
single file, like ants
and waited our turn

I'd practice my cursive
in the dry Nevada dirt
while random men
talked to my mom
she'd laugh at their jokes
and give them a phone number
to a phone
we didn't own
and when they would walk away
she'd shoot me a look
that told me
my L's still looked like my E's

when it was finally our turn
the beautiful girls from the church
would hand us loaves of bread,
blocks of cheese, noodles
and a few rolls of toilet paper
once, I even showed one of the girls
a toothless smile

for an extra loaf of bread
but I didn't like to use that one too often
because I knew one day, I'd be older
and I wouldn't want them
to remember that
about me

by the time we got back to our trailer
it would be lunchtime
we'd make 3 grilled cheese
one each,
and then we'd split the third

the best part of having another half
is that even if you don't want it,
you're just happy it's there

2. my mother sobbed
in the office of my school
and again on the bus ride home
I could feel the blood in my face freezing
as strangers stared at us
I kept my head tucked as close
to my belly button as possible
trying to make sense of the conversations
playing out in my head

an older boy
made me a target
for years
but something in the way that it hurt,
changed
and so, I brought a brick to school
and threw it at the back of his head
during lunch
and by the time
the ringing in my ear
had stopped,
they followed my size 6
bloody shoe print
to the janitors closet
and found me
on the cold wet floor

my mother cried through dinner
and even after she thought I was asleep

I heard her open the tiny ziplock bag
she kept beneath her pillow
containing all of my dads last worn items
and she called out for his help
as she breathed the contents of his memory,
deep into her lungs
and I laid still with my eyes shut
praying
that I'd never
have to open them again

3. when I was small,
I would bounce my rubber bones
off the rocks near the river
and on the summer
after I grew my first armpit hair
I thought that if I opened
my mouth wide enough,
I could drink the river dry

my friends cheered me on
while I held my face
beneath the surface
but the river, as it does,
overcame me
and dragged me all the way to the stream
behind my house

my mother saw me through the window
sloshing towards the back door
and scolded me
with a spatula
and I only looked up
in hopes of seeing neighbors
peeking through their blinds
but everyone around us
had a job and stayed in school

the urge to say something sharp enough
to burst her single parenting bubble
sat on my tongue
like a passenger
and when I found the space to speak,
I let the words rush out of me
and prayed for the worst
but my mother stood in silence
as I dripped onto the garden
eager to be punished

she pointed towards the house
with a silent scream
so I hung my head
and obeyed

I made faces at the boy
in the yellow bathroom mirror
and held my hands beneath the scalding water
while I counted to 10
and even still,
 nothing

Idle Hands

"you're edging god out"
she said, under her breath
reassuring her point
that I should drown
all these thoughts
in the shallow water
when in truth
I wasn't ready
to wash the sin off,
not yet
and though
my wrists
were too sore
to pray,
I listened to her speak to god
as if I weren't there
and I played my part
like everyone else

Night Drive

she keeps the windows down
as she drives fast into the night
her hair in a violent dance
and the headlights wash out
the little bit of red on her cheeks
my white knuckles choke the seatbelt
like a street dog to a bone
a song comes on the radio
and it breaks her heart
her foot gets heavier on the gas pedal
as she sings the important parts
out loud

we pass the old playground
where I'd chipped my tooth
chasing the girl,
this girl
years ago
and the irony makes me blush

as I become one with the seat
pretending to feel complacent,
I try to sneak a glance at her

but every darting eye
is met with the fear of not witnessing
the very thing
that will kill me

the headlights pull us further into the night
past our friends houses
the thought of them asleep
in their teenage bodies
dreaming of other teenage bodies
almost made me ashamed
knowing
I'd never wonder
again

the car lifts from the warm concrete
and she looks over at me
as the chorus drowns out the sound of the trees
whipping past us

the car hovers over our neighborhood
and the moon positions itself between
the small gap of our faces

she stares into me,
half silhouetted,
truthful and intense
leans in close
and presses her face into mine
her warm skin melts
and pours into my hands
as I hold her

floating 1,000 feet in the air
I felt the weight of the world
in the words of the song
as they tried to pull us back to our youth
heavy as they were,
it could never be enough

Summer Stained Sweet and Salty

the salt from your sweat
burned my lips
in the backseat of my uncles old car
while the summer peeked
through the cracked window
at our exposed skin
sticking to the leather seats
tangled up
in one another

Glass

they painted the word "caution"
down my spine
a parting gift from the artists that made me
I grew older and when others learned to feel
nothing
I wanted to feel it all
so every heavy hand
felt worth it in the end
but time eventually called my number
told me "baby come on home"
but it was too late
the cold air was blowing
through the shattered remains of myself
in the attic of my parents house
and with the reminder no longer looming
I let the weight of the world
consume me

The Greatest Memory I Have
of Feeling Somewhat Decent

the leaves were brittle
and cracked underneath my stride
15 years old
and everything was getting better
I was arrogant,
I was cocky
I was beautiful
and not just on the exterior
I felt it too
bright green
or golden yellow

I could've looked you in the eyes
if we spoke
I could've listened
and not felt obligated
to fill the silent cracks
in small talk

that was when the flame
was buried deep
and safe
but the world is cruel
and pulled it right out of my soul

and I was too afraid
to watch the flame die,
so I let it consume me
and now,
15 years older than I was,
I'm still sifting through the ashes

I've Come to Accept
That Outrunning Yourself
Only Leads to Seeing
the Worst Things Happen First

I don't know how
but somewhere along the way
I became afraid of the world
I even doubt my own shadows loyalty
I need to find a way
to get myself back together
because I'm really fucking losing grip

July's rain
used to cool my cooked skin
and now, I rush my dog
to finish shitting on our walk
when the rain clouds gather
over my cold shoulder

A Stepping Stone so Shall I Remain

I've been a passenger in her life
for years now
the afterthought,
the moral memory,
the crowning jewel
of the *worst* case scenario
she held me like a burden
when she held me like a child
a debt, I'll never fully repay

the guest that

never left

We Get Better but Do We Ever?

I used to need an excuse
to tuck my head into my chest
but the weight just sits there now
on a rusted hinge
from the reheated cold coffee,
swinging
in and out of misery
the worms in my belly stir
as I cry into the void
so I'm gonna attempt
to put some words on this page
and pray they make some sense
 pray they make me better

I used to need an excuse to fall apart
but now,
I sit back
and wait my turn

I've been dreaming of the moment
I'd fall apart
my whole life
is it so strange
to want to go out
with a bang?
to be a balloon
tied to a cactus
waiting for the wind
or stuck inside a television screen
with the audience hooked like fish
on the other side
the thought alone makes my fingernails cold
but my belly warm
no liquor could ever compare
to the type of numb
that comes from dreaming
of your own escape
not death
but a silent bow
and a proper exit

validated

so I've painted myself yellow
and watch the sun
through envious eyes

waiting
each day
for my chance to burn out

there's no room for me
so I sit
in my skin
and out
of my mind
watching the cars go by
leaving whatever's left
for everyone else

Manifest

I finally washed
all of my sadness off in the shower
but it found its way into the silence hovering
between us
and chokes the life out of our plants
so we watch the leaves
from green to yellow
then shrivel up and die

too many self help books
have me searching for meaning
in the passing of time
but if simple silence is the friend of comfort
maybe the happiest people
don't have much to say
when a thing dies

I know you care
when I don't ask you to
but a part of me wishes
 you wouldn't
in fact,
it might be easier
 if you didn't
because there is no answer
to why I am,
the way I am
or for what I've become
and falling apart in front of an audience
has always been my least favorite fantasy
 so I plead
that you turn your head
 instead of wiping my tears
and push me away
 instead of pulling me close
because it's gonna be a long night,
I can feel it
and you've got work in the morning

Quarantine

the last half of the year
locked inside of myself
pretending that I can make magic
in the same room
I cry myself to sleep

The Critic

selling a piece of paper
to a burning fire
just so you could say
you were a part
of something

I open up my mouth
and hear my fathers voice
and it breaks my heart
that a man
who never left a room unturned
would be immortalized
in the sound
of my rage
and so,
every time
I feel the heat in my face rise
shame creeps closely behind
as I carry the torch of a man
who only ever used it
to set his own children on fire

Control

I lay beneath
the crashing waves
inside my head
with open arms
this place,
it isn't good for me
but it's all
that I've got

her skin was wet paper
wrapped around blue veins
sick with rage
as we pulled her onto the ship

it took four men to contain her
as she convulsed
on the cold wet floor of the bow
one of the wranglers
tied a rope 'round her waist
and hoisted her up in the air
rest of the crew
pulled the anchored chains
from the black sea water
and the boat lunged toward land
men dogpile to take photos with the catch,
afterwards retiring below deck
to celebrate

"how do you think we should split her up"
one man spat
wiping the foam from his upper lip
"I SHOULD GET MORE CAUSE IT WAS
ME SHE BIT!"
shouted a wrangler
waving his bloody stump in the air

I snuck out between the argument
back onto the deck
where she dangled upside down

I pulled at the rope stuffed between her bite
she inhaled the cold sea air
hovering between us
her pupils focused on me
until her breath thinned
"American?" she let out on the exhale
I didn't say a thing,
avoided her gaze
by staring into the blood pooling beneath her
"please let me go" she begged
"let me go and I'll remember you at the end of
the world"
"end of the world?"
I looked over my shoulder to make sure
any of the crew hadn't stumbled out
"I'm just a hired gun okay?"
I pleaded,
practically whispering
"I just needed to feed my daughters..."
she was quiet
as I stared out into the darkness
unfolding all around us

the ship carved through
the black water beneath
and the salt
from the crashing waves
wrapped itself
around the rim of my beer
and chapped my lips
"I'm sorry it's gotta be like this" I leveled,
thinking of my youngest Ashley
"your fate is outta my hands,
the scientists paid for these ships,
they cut my checks..."
her thoughts swimming
in the burgundy night sky above her head
"what will happen to me?"
she asked, soft and afraid
I craned my neck over my shoulder again
still no one,
just me, her, and the moon
"I don't know"
I admitted,
and I meant it
tears fell up her face and made tiny ripples in
her blood
the defeat was setting in

"one day the sea will consume everyone and
everything" she hissed
I crouched down
and put the rope back in her mouth

"if I'm lucky, I'll be long gone before it does"

I couldn't sleep that night
just layed in my bunk
and listened,
as the waves cried out

for their baby

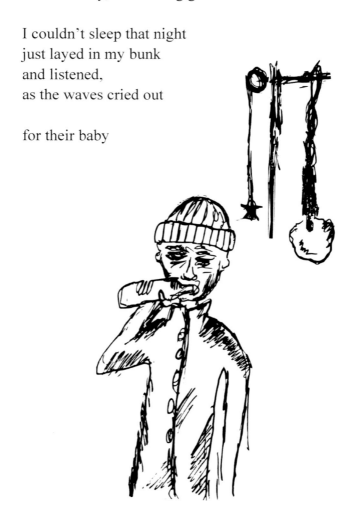

without bringing on concern
how can I let them know
there's an emptiness in me
that doesn't need to be exploited

a whole life of experience
but the sadness came
and filled in all the gaps
of the parts
I can't remember

when all I ever wanted was to grow
the world wrapped a blanket
around my shivering teenage body
and threw me back in the ocean

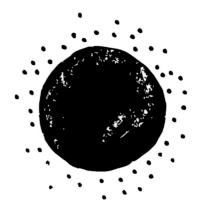

Respect the Process

I'm afraid to confess
to everyone I love
that I'm stumbling through life
in fear they'd feel robbed
of the patience they kept
or the time that it cost
I just hope in the end
they'll forgive that I lost

VA-LA-FL

I've been thinking about
going somewhere nice
where the breeze flows through my hair
and I don't have to drink to be seen
by the world

or maybe somewhere quiet
where I could be invisible
unwatched
complacent even

it's just,
I keep creating these scenarios in my head
that leave me feeling half empty
when they dissolve
and half empty
is starting to feel like it's not enough
to get me where I'm going

and where I'm going
I don't know
but I'll never make it
with what I've got

so I've gotta make a change

fix my soul,
heal the hurt
and maybe,
 going somewhere new

will help me find the starting line

the sun was lashing down
on the necks
of pink and purple pantone families
in the backyard
clumped together like clusters of ants
extended arms
attached to paper plates
a safe place for the slightly burnt aroma
hovering in the air,
to land

the children splashed water
on anyone in proximity
some parents willingly walked closer
to the pool's edge
as the sun rose higher in the sky
the water poured onto the hot concrete
camouflaging it only for a second
before drinking it all in

mark was the host
and a fellow holy man
the holiest next to God,

 some would've told ya

he ran service every Sunday and Wednesday
and hosted events out on his land
every month

he was a good guy

mark and his son moved into town
after his wife passed,
he sold the house they built together
and moved further down south,
 closer to God
the love he had for his wife
only came second
to the love of his creator

quiet, yet strong
waved hello to everyone he saw
and was a damn good father
a looker, too, if you asked the ladies in town

god gifted him, and he blessed us
with his word and his kindness
but eventually,

God takes everything back

mark maintained his grill
while the party unfolded around him
the kids splashed in the pool
the dads talked amongst dads
the moms the moms
a table full of box made baked goods
from suggestively sympathetic mothers
grew taller than the scrap pile
of burnt chicken legs and pork chops,
a holy man,
but a distracted one

"WHIRLPOOL," a tiny voice screamed
and all the kids rushed to the center of the pool
the goal being, everyone in the water
walks at the same pace in a circle,
spinning whoever was lucky enough
to be stuck in the center

"DAAD, look, i'M GONNA do the
WHORLDpool"
Daniel pressed off the bottom of the pool to see
over the kids circling him
but Mark was coating the chicken in another
layer of barbecue sauce
the kids circled faster and faster,
and before he could reach his big toe

to the chalky bottom, he lost his footing and
spun under

"DINNER!" mark beamed,
shutting the lid on the grill with intent
the entire backyard snapped into a cadence
wrinkled kids broke the chain
and climbed out of the pool in a frenzy

the stampede pulled Daniel
to the deep end of the pool
and before he could lash his arms
towards the sunlight
flickering onto the surface above him,
 fear consumed him
tiny bubbles floated to the top of the water
and burst in the sunlight

Mark made the last two hotdogs
for him and his son
coating the crisped skin
with a thick layer of mustard and ketchup

"Daniel!,"he called out to the backyard

the talking heads ceased

and the chewing and the gnawing
and the crunching of potato chips
came to lull
"now I know I made you guys wait a while,
but that doesn't mean the party has to stop."
he said, turning from the condiment table
"where's the exci…"
a sudden shriek
sliced the stagnant summer air
followed by another

Daniel was face down
floating in the pool
slowly spinning in place

Mark dove into the pool
and pulled his son's body
to the edge of the water
he pressed on his tiny chest
and forced his own panicked breath
into his sons' blue lips

the neighbors looked down upon
the boy
and his father

as he cradled his child

sobbing
his tears sank deep
beneath his sons cooked skin

Mark buried his son in the fall
 sold his house, and the land
and moved into a motel
somewhere down the road

that winter, it snowed 6 days straight
and on the 7th, Mark bought a handgun

he sat silently on the edge of the bed
in his dim-lit room
clutching the well-worn leather book
from his bedside table
and holding the cold steel barrel
up to his temple

"oh, holy father..."
                        his tears drowned out the
rest of his prayer
the silence finally came
as the frost on the window
thawed from his blood

there was no news report
no sermon at the church
the town never mentioned Mark, his son,
or any of the others that came here
looking for something
they weren't ready to find

Self-Employed

I try to dignify
the desire to touch myself
before getting anything done
as *self-love*
but the nirvana
drains out of me
like a low swinging pinata
when I see my half-naked body
in the mirror
making me feel
like a stranger
 in my own house
so I cover-up
reheat the abandoned cup of coffee
next to an open laptop
with another unfinished poem
about

sex

Vo·yeur

we go out for drinks
and end up in the backseat
of our car
kissing slow and hard
our bodies flicker
in the headlights passing by
where all the world
could watch me undress you
and somewhere
between the rush
and the reward
we melt into the seats
and the night
goes by
unaware

Whatever You Want,
Let Me Be That, Please.

she told me there's a fire
buried deep inside of her
and I want it to consume me
she puts me in my place
and rips me out of my mind
oh how I beg
to be
her dog

To Us,

she loved to be loved
on the bed that we bought
when the band started doing okay
 time and space
could only ever make
a love like what we made
but we had it
and tried
to give it away
yet still
it always came back,
 to us

Money

the more I have
the more I want to fuck
and that makes me feel
like a terribly empty person
the type of man you hear about in the news
that gets a fast car and crashes into a wall
a week later
the irony always being that they live so fast,
the only thing that could kill them
was stopping
suddenly
but it's not like that
because I grew up a bum,
a roach to society
and I need to spend money on things
that make me feel like I won't leave this place
with the filth
that I see in the mirror
so I wanna make a lot of money
spoil her
and her friends
so when she climbs on top of me
I can close my eyes and fantasize
about her robbing me blind

Love Lost

I used to lay underneath a stranger
while she'd cover my face
with her hands, as she got off
shielding me from the car crash
unfolding between us
her desire to be fulfilled
coddled my fear of being alone
for years
and though she rode me with intent,
underneath her grip,
I closed my eyes
and tried not to visualize
the insignificance of two people fucking
mostly clothed,
on a Tuesday afternoon
  she loved me,
  until she didn't
and then she'd stumble into the shower
where the hot water
washed the memory of me
right off of her
and I'd lay in my mind
in the emptiness of our bed,
wrapped up in whatever
she left me with

In the End I Realized
That Nothing Makes Me Feel
More Accomplished
Than Pleasing Others

placebo,
that's what my best friend
in 7th grade told me they were
"they also make your dick soft"
so I went home
and flushed my Wellbutrin
down the toilet
and never looked back
I lied for an entire year
and flushed them all away
the same year I got
my first patch of pubic hair
the same year I had a panic attack
mid first under bra experience
where her parents
would have to call my mom
wanting an explanation
for the convulsing, half naked teen boner
hiding out in their guest bathroom

I'm an alright fuck
everything else about me
isn't really worth bragging about
but, consistency carries with it
a sense of pride
and pride will kill us all in the end
but I'll be happy to leave
with the one thing given to me in this life
determination,
my professional navigator tells me
to spin it as
and not the desire to feed others
while starving myself

I fall in love with being desired by strangers
a gift given in passing glances
in coffee shops and self-checkout lines
I want to be fucked
more than I want to be loved
a family curse
but the thought of being used
in someone's fleeting passion
is a rush of dopamine
only ever paid for in sessions

floating

Grow

we fell apart separately
and put ourselves back
together

Cold Woman

unused like that teapot
her mother got us,
that's what I try to convince her I am
but she's heard this line enough
throughout the years
stitched into my many forms
of self destruction
"quiet"
       she says,
              before the fuse can catch
"why don't you use that fire in your mouth
  on something else"

Yellow Bird, Why Do You Sing the Blues?

my favorite nights with you
are the ones where you let slip
those moments of reverie
as you sing between the voices
on the radio

there's something in the way
you speak my name
that doesn't make me hate the sound
and for the first time
in a long time
you make me want to clean up my head
and make some room,
for you

I Don't Want to Take Your Fire, I Want to Be Consumed

I'm the type of person
to tell you
that I want you to destroy me
then fall apart
when you do

Enjoy the Ride

the hardest part
of loving someone else
is that they never tell you
how to love,
someone else
so if it comes,
try to let it in
and don't apologize
for a goddamn thing

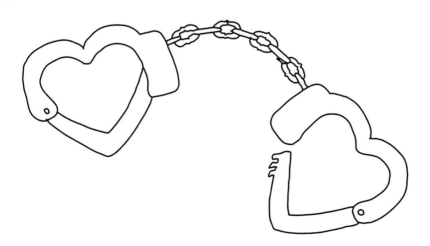

I swivel the toothpaste around my teeth
and sneak glances of her body
through the swirling steam
in the mirror
after flossing
and somewhere in between
picking and prodding
at the thinning skin beneath my eyes
I won't ask her if she thinks
I'm starting to look
as old as I am,
not tonight

the water moves down her body
and washes away the soapy layer
revealing her polished legs
in spite of myself,
I carry on the conversation
and nose through her shelf
of coveted serums and oils
hunting for an effect
I could cling to
brighten, depuff,
moisturizing, oil-free,
everything
but reversing
the damage is done

and time itself
cannot be nourished
nor rejuvenated
small talk rolls over
the fogged glass panel between us
as I sulk back to the mirror and
pluck the contacts from my eyes
staring back at the blurry stranger
somewhat satisfied

A Mothers Moment

she opens up the window
letting the smoke
escape the lungs
buried beneath her naked chest
dragging out the last little bit of clarity
through pursed lips

the dryer cycle ends
and the baby sleeps
two rooms away

she pulls the warm beige sweater
from the dryer
gargles the mouthwash
tucked behind the detergent
and listens
to the rise and fall
of the tiny little chest
through the baby monitor

they breathe in sync
as she presses it closer to her ear
drowning out the rest
of everything else

sinking

Throwing the Controller Doesn't Make it Any Easier

"do you feel like you could die alone?",
she asked
between the minutes
of the hours that passed us by
spending all of our money on plants to burn
or plants to let
              be
                  burned
      by the sun
     it's a shame
   how often
we ruin the things
we never learned to fix

I kissed her lips
and tasted the sadness on them
where others had been
before me
so I panicked
and tried to fix a problem
that never needed to be fixed
in the first place
but a sadness like that,
lingers
and it spreads
so I cut off my own lips
and I placed them on hers
but the salt from her tears
made them fall from her face
so now,
we just sit,
in silence

Hopeless

when I fall in love
I become the other person
and count the months like spare change
forgetting that once you lose yourself
in someone else,
the love itself
will suffocate
like being trapped beneath a wall
with too many coats of paint
but if no one ever learns to love me
who will protect
what I can't
seem to take,
you either lose yourself in others
or lose yourself along the way

some fall
because the chance
of someone waiting at the bottom
is worth more
than holding on
for dear life

vacant words that fill
the space between them
conversations so small
they barely make a sound
she waits for the television
to sing him to sleep
and turns towards the wall,
it's plainness
more exhilarating
than the mass of weight
beside her

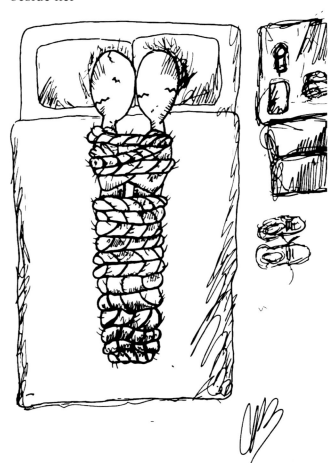

why is there no heart in the words
when you lie through your teeth?
you've embraced the fact that you're going to
tell me,
so where's your dignity?

the hardest part of knowing
is for months I called myself crazy
and ruined pieces of myself
while you sat with me in silence
and I tasted it on your lips
and smelled it on your skin
 you were there
  but not with me

you told me
the pressure of forcing all of your ideas
into one set of bones
was destroying your ability
to be present
yet here we are
 present
and you make me feel
like I woke up beside a stranger,
a set of bones
I protected
more than my own

Salty Skin

his sheets
keep their secret
like a joke
between friends
and I pray
that the smell
of her hair
wraps itself around his throat
like an extension cord

The Warmth of a Burning Building
Is Better Than the Chill
of an Empty House

she doesn't think she's human
cause paranoia didn't wake up beside her
and now,
because there's nothing to fear,
she's feeling blue

blue like the sky that hangs around
a little longer
to watch the moon and sun meet one another
and not like the paint that dripped
from her hands
when the walls felt the wrath
of her broken heart

she sits at the kitchen table,
loneliness joins her
a splinter,
bullied deep into her memory

she closes her eyes
and lets him in
swallowing the coffee
before it can cool

it grips at her throat
on the way down

shame,
she feels
but the warmth
of a burning building
is better
than the chill
of an empty house

death

Horny for Chaos

when the night terrors
still made me piss the bed
I used to ask god
for an answer
or a purpose
and revisit the flawed skin
in hopes that it would deem a response

but only silence ever came
and it hovered above in the dark
until I'd slip into the same dream
I'd been having for months

where I'm on a ship
surrounded by women
 all resembling my babysitter
and treasure chests full of fruit- roll-ups
but the sides of my vessel
had been blown to pieces
letting in the open sea around me

 self destructive,
that's what my therapist said
when I revisited the dream
in his leather green chair

too ashamed to mention
the other symptoms

like spending the first half
of 6th grade
tucking the pirate led erection
behind the belt loops
of my cargo shorts

It's not even winter yet
and everything is dying

I see it
when I look in the mirror
but death reminds me
not to flatter myself
and that the man in the mirror
is a stranger
 that I invited in

the sun rises and falls outside
for everyone else
as I sink deeper into the cold bath water
searching for meaning
in the little bit of light
crawling in from underneath
the locked door

"this day will end"
is the only remedy I have
before confusion and loss
take over
and I welcome the war
in my mind and on my body

the adult version of myself
or, what became of all that eagerness
to please others
begs to be broken into tiny pieces,
stomped into a fine powder
and washed away
if
their eyes start to rain
when nothing but a breeze
 passes through my apartment

scenarios play out
like silent bombs
in the quiet corners of my mind
so I tell myself
"this day will end"
and it brings me comfort
if nothing else,
at least,
 it always does

Reaper

I was on a park bench,
head swimming in something dark enough
to drown in
when a man in tattered black clothes found me
and told me how happy he was
that I'd lost my way
so I asked him to sit with me
if only for or a little while,
at least until the sun rose
but he shook his head
and told me there'd be no point
to wait until morning

shame
in the presence of the moon
is romantic
but underneath a rising sun,
it's only shame

he put his hand on my shoulder,
wiped the tears from my eyes
and his thin voice
crackled in my ear like television static

good n i g h t,

he whispered

the silence came,
I closed my eyes
begging it would finally be
the last time

I feel distant here
with everyone around

and I know that control
comes from asking for help
but I'm almost afraid to be fixed

if not this,
what else?

if not the journey to overcome
 whatever it is that I've become,

what else do I have?

when I feel the most loved
 is when I feel the most guilt
so I bury the worst parts of me
deep inside my head
and leave the door half-open
praying that they'll follow
so that I can keep creating
so that I can stay here
with the rest of you

the problem
and the solution,
 the self destruction
it only ever rests
when I bleed it into the words of a song
or the words on a page

so Ollie, if you're reading this,
thanks

IS THERE ANYTHING LEFT FOR THE REST OF US?

"Trailer Trash"
from the upcoming **"Trailer Trash, stories from the shadows of the Las Vegas strip"**
written by **Oliver Baxxter**

I knew we were poor. Just not truly how poor.
I mean, on a scale of wearing clothes from the
Gap to wearing a hoodie stolen from a
goodwill donation bin, I was the one wearing
the hoodie. I knew the government paid for our
groceries, and my dads' paycheck almost paid
our rent each month. I knew that my mom took
the bus to work every day and that we only got
Nickelodeon because of the hissing wires that
hung between ours and our neighbor Becky's
trailer. We were a lot of things, but I never
knew we were the p-word. Not until the first
day of fourth grade. Ryan Michael Shoemaker
looked me right in the eyes and called me
"trailer trash." My head swelled into a pink
balloon as the entire class burst into
laughter--even the other poor kids. I sank
beneath my desk like chewed-up bubblegum
and spent the rest of the day there.

My embarrassment rode beside me on the way
home from school and tucked me in that night.
There's no pride in being a poor kid, none.

Ryan lived on the other side of poverty and
brought a packed lunch every single day. He
had unwritten permission to bully anyone at
school because he had an actual house and an
even haircut. I hated him because he was
everything that I wanted to be, except for the
being an asshole part. Or the fucked up dad
part.

Back when we still stood in the lunch line
together, he had asked me to come to his
Denver Broncos-themed birthday party. Only a
weirdo wouldn't jump at the opportunity to be
within the walls of a middle-class family. I did
push-ups the three days leading up to the event.
No reason whatsoever, one of those "potential
ground zero anxiety development moments,"
I'd later pay a therapist to translate.

I stood on his doorstep with sweaty palms,
almost ripping the dollar store wrapping paper
in my clammy grip. The door opened, and the
man behind it was the same size as my father

but wore it differently. "RYAN!" the man called out to the house, and seconds later, he appeared. The walls of their living room vomited blue and orange streamers in every direction. There was a cake, perfectly un-homemade, and the dining room table buckled beneath the presents. The kitchen was its own room, with its own windows overlooking a massive, beautifully lain astroturf backyard.

For a moment, I felt like one of the few living things the Nevada sun couldn't take away. His house was the first non-trailer or extended stay hotel I'd ever been inside. Reality rained down when Ryan's mom asked me to leave my shoes at the door. The sobering moment that'd have me spend the rest of the night hiding the toes that peeked through my holey socks.

A *normal* person would've taken the socks off instead of hiding behind various props all night. A *normal* person wouldn't have painted their feet in sharpie days before. I developed the habit of going absolutely all the way with things early in life.

I had been shamefully hiding my neon feet from my family for four days. The same feet would designate me as the living target at a ten-year-olds football-themed birthday party. The anxiety push-ups only made my arms sore and more prone to be sucker-punched, which in the end, really does live up to its name. After playing various versions of Ryan's friends beating my ass in the backyard all day, it was time for all the kids to gather and watch him pretend to like our gifts. A kid buying presents for another kid is never a good idea, the stakes are high, and someone's feelings always get hurt in the end. The first present was a bike Ryan's dad wheeled out from one of the guest rooms. I felt robbed of the natural progression of these things. Small gift, shitty gift, definitely returned gift- THEN the heavy hitters come out. One by one, we waited in anticipation to see what he would open next. It's hard to fake excitement for someone else when folding pieces of carelessly tossed wrapping paper into your pockets. A young enthusiast of elite gift wrapping utensils? No. Simply a klepto with a hunger for quality. Later they'd call this being a hipster, but then, just a sad little monster.

I was drooling like a hyena over a finally abandoned carcass by the time Ryan got to my gift. Two packs of skittles and a bag of water balloons. The room laughed, and so did Ryan.

The night eventually went on; I ate more than I could, and then I ate some more. I was the last of all the kids to leave because I needed Ryan's dad to drive me home. His mom wrapped up the rest of the grilled hotdogs and cheeseburgers on a plate for me to take while he flashed his high beams through the front window from the paved driveway. I swallowed my pride with yet another tongue-staining royal blue cupcake before asking Ryan to ride along because I didn't like being alone with adults.

Ryans' mom poured herself a glass from the bottle she kept underneath the kitchen sink as we closed the actual wooden door on the last night of our potential friendship. Somewhere in-between, his dad yelling at people for not using turn signals and slamming his heavy hands down on the horn, Ryan's soccer competition got brought up.

I made another mental note after:
scrub feet in bleach, to ask my family to sign
me up for soccer. I could tell he didn't want to
talk about it, but his father was persistent, like
most. After four traffic lights worth of Ryan
back-peddling and de-escalating, his dad
stopped the car on the side of the road. He
turned the top half of his body around so that
we could see the fire burning in his eyes. "Stop
being a little fucking girl." He said, somewhere
behind his teeth. Ryan cried the rest of the way
in the darkness of the backseat. Every time
we'd pass a streetlight, I could see his face
glistening. That was the last time I saw him the
entire summer and the first time I had ever
pitied him.

Before school started back up, my mom and I
had developed a habit of staying up late on
Sundays. We would take my stepdad's work
van and drive it to the parking lot next to
Goodwill. The one closer to the cleaner
neighborhoods, where Ryan lived. She'd leave
the car running but cut the headlights. The
streets were quiet, and the only other people
out were the sinners. Every Sunday, people felt
more compelled to donate to the bins outside of

the store. Dressers, lamps, broken toys, etc. but the real treasure, the creme de la creme, were the big black trash bags: piled high, like a plastic utopia.

We'd make sure the coast was clear; she'd nod, then I'd haul ass sprinting through the dark empty parking lot towards the donation bins illuminated under a single light post. Just me and the moths floating beneath its glow. I had developed a feel for the name-brand trash bags, the kind that didn't rip when you ran with them. My hands were small; I couldn't grab more than two at a time, one of my first encounters with shame.

I felt perfectly juvenile running back towards my mother, waiting, smiling, with the trunk popped. Some wouldn't call this back-to-school shopping, and that's okay. On the way home, she'd tell me how proud of me she was. She worked all day, so I didn't see her much. I liked spending this time with my mom because it made me feel like I was more than just another mouth to feed.

I'd tell her I was proud of her too, and then she'd cry and turn the radio up as we drove home.

When we'd get back to our trailer, we'd start by sorting everything into piles on the living room floor. I loved seeing all the things people didn't *want* anymore. Clothes, worn only one to four-ish times, tossed because they didn't fit, or had a small stain, or a "practically unnoticeable hole that no one would ever even see." Pictures of strangers, still in their frames. Their donors, too ashamed to remove the photograph from its home, but not the person's memory from their own. Socks, board games, sometimes even money. I'd ask my mom why people would ever donate money, and she'd tell me because they were stupid. After we'd shop, we would rebag the wearables and leave them in the laundromat for other families, like the trailer trash robin hoods. It wasn't much, but sometimes a hand-me-down could be the thing that lifts someone else back up.

Seven days after mom and I's last seasonal escapade, I was standing in the middle of the classroom wearing Ryan Michael Shoemakers' old clothes. On the first day. Of fourth grade. I couldn't make sense of all the words that waited to rush past the gaps in my teeth. I was poor when he invited me to his birthday, and I was poor when he squeezed my hand in the backseat of his dads' car. What changed? I was embarrassed, and even though I felt like climbing on top of my desk and telling everyone how he cried to the sound of his dad's voice, it didn't feel right. I cried too. I cried when I got out of the car that night after his birthday. I cried when my dad had surgery on his heart. I even cried when Mufasa died in The Lion King. Not because he was gone, but because, like Simba, I felt ashamed for being alive when my dad died too. I couldn't find the words to defend myself because I knew that he was right; I *was* trailer trash.

The teacher silenced everyone, eventually. But I still felt their eyes raking at my back and clawing at my weird-shaped ears. I watched the walls and counted the remaining hours from my desk, forcing back the tears that gathered in the back of my eyes, praying they wouldn't pile high enough to pour out.

When I got home, my mother had washed all my new clothes and folded them into neat piles. I pressed my face into the clouds of laundry detergent that remained on the surface—trying to breathe in deep enough to convince myself that they weren't once someone else's but mine. Almost.

I closed my eyes and let the tears fall onto the pile of another boys' jeans.

Oliver Baxxter is a touring musician, singer/songwriter, and poet. His previous work includes You, Me, and the Moon, which was widely received by his audience base as an independent release. Currently, Baxxter is crafting his first collection of short stories, satirically centered around the Las Vegas trailer park that raised him. He draws inspiration from and paints a new light on the tropes of youth, mental health, and relationships from a unique perspective.
His band Broadside, has three studio albums and have been on multiple world tours.

-

Baxxter resides in Orlando, Florida where he watches the sunset each night with his fiance and their miniature dachshund, Leo.

Contact:
Oliverbaxxter@gmail.com
@Oliverbaxxter

Acknowledgments

*I'd like to start by thanking my fiance **Sara**; without you, all I'd be is a cup of cold coffee with some hot sauce swirling at the top. You give me a reason to write, laugh, and to be here; I love you.*

***To my family**, I love us and what we have left, and I think, after some time, it's all gonna make sense.*

***Dom**, (I call you at 7am, I call you at 5pm and I've called you at 4 in the morning. I don't think you know how much it means that you always answer, thank you for that) **Pat**, (we all sat around and cried on your birthday. Everyone minus you. I love that and you), **Jeff**, (we sink so deep into our own skin just to remind ourselves we're still here. we're sacks of emotions, fatherless and a little on the shorter side, that's okay. It's safer down here anyways) **Alex and Ryan**, (we've grown into our adult minds and bodies together, how the fuck did we get here?), **Ava**, (please don't read this book, your sister plays a significant role), **Marie** (live. life. Big.)*

Madison *(please stay a champion of the world, you make me so proud)* **Andrew**, *(thanks for saving my life with that email)*, **Lauren**, **Mia**, *(one more lap?)*, **Aaron**, *(Leo chewed up the DVD you let me borrow, and I couldn't think of a better way to tell you)*, **Sarah W.**, **Alex**, *(handsome and sad, your gift and your curse)*, **Niles**, *(proud of you, always, Yucca St. forever)*, **Maddie**, *(thanks for believing in me)*, **Abbie**, *(a world apart but are we really?)*, **Shawn Keith**, *(you saved me from myself many times and believed in the music from the jump, thank you for that)* **Ryan** *"Tuck"*, *(you made me feel like I deserved a seat at the table, shoutout Featured X)*, **Lisa**, *(you gifted me with a skill, that I'll take to the grave, thank you for trusting me with it)* **Alexis** *(1 of 6 good people in LA)*, **Jack Rogers** *(I remember when you first interviewed me, and really, I just wanted to ask questions about you instead, look at us now)* **Gav**, *(if there's anything good left here, you deserve it all)*

To all the other creatives, doers, and over-thinkers that I've had the privilege of working with on this project or anywhere else on this trip, I'm a better man having shared the space with you.

thanks for reading.